A PIECE OF STRING?

A low flame looks like this

A medium looks like

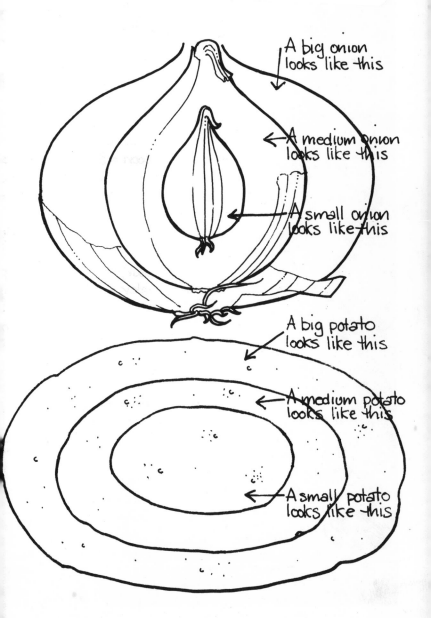

A big onion looks like this

A medium onion looks like this

A small onion looks like this

A big potato looks like this

A medium potato looks like this

A small potato looks like this

How
to Survive
in the Kitchen

by the same author

How
to Survive
in the Kitchen

KATHARINE WHITEHORN

with drawings by Larry

EYRE METHUEN

First published in 1979 by Eyre Methuen Ltd
11 New Fetter Lane, London EC4P 4EE

Text © 1979 by Katharine Whitehorn
Drawings and captions © 1979 by Larry
Cover design by Larry

Printed in Great Britain by
Butler & Tanner Ltd
Frome and London

ISBN 0 413 39800 5

British Library Cataloguing in Publication Data

Whitehorn, Katharine
    How to survive in the kitchen.
    1. Cookery
    641.5   TX652
    ISBN 0-413-39800-5

Acknowledgments

My grateful thanks are due to Liz Ray for giving me the Apple
Cream Pudding and the Horse Picnic; to Jean Robertson for her
cold yoghurt soup; to my mother-in-law, Ann Lyall, and my
sister-in-law, Barbara Lyall, for all sorts of helpful tips; to my
mother for teaching me how to make mince and gravy, among
other things; to Virginia Bredin for the Bredin Bodge and invalu-
able help with the whole book; and above all to my husband
Gavin Lyall for the Chinese Meal and for putting up so gamely
with all my experiments.

CONTENTS

PART SIX: Branching out

Pastry, like horses and small children, knows if you're afraid of it and plays up accordingly.

Evelyn Board

PART ONE

How did I get here?

INTRODUCTION

Some people are born cooks; some achieve good cooking; and some have cooking thrust upon them. The fact that there are so many more people who get stuck with providing meals than actually want to cook is the reason for this book.

Time was, when only those who could cook, did cook. Unless you knew how to make bread, how to truss a fowl or soak the salt bacon to make it half-way edible, you had to find someone else who did – or starve. Not now. There are enough tins and packets around to give the illusion that anyone can run up a meal any time.

Once, a girl would learn some skills at her mother's elbow, then start cooking for two and progress gradually through baby-food to family cooking. Now she may find she goes straight from a candle-lit supper for two (which she can just about manage) to coping with her bloke's four children by his first marriage every Sunday. Or she joins five others in a flat, and cooks for the whole crew once a week. Husbands, who once reckoned to give up for good once they'd exchanged their grotty gas ring for marriage and a mortgage on a decent kitchen, now find abruptly that they are in the firing line again. The wife has gone back to work, and he has to cook on Tuesdays when she's late home. Or she's gone back to Mother, and he has to feed the children. Or back to Nature, so that he cooks in self-defence against all that wheatgerm and brown rice. Cooking, nowadays, can strike anyone at any time.

And you can see the rich assortment of people it has struck. There is the splendid random cook who seems to grab the first six things she sees, throws them in a pan with an unmeasured quantity of water, forgets all about it and produces the most ambrosial dish of pasta you ever tasted. There's the meticulous cook who knows to the last gramme how much of everything he has to put into a dish, and achieves it all with a clean draining board and spotless cuffs; the only snag is that if he cannot get exactly the right herb or spice for the dish in question he – and it's usually a he – is (like other fetishists) unable to perform at all.

There are fewer, thank goodness, of the Good Plain Cook types around these days: the ones who thought that beef roasted till it was grey, sprouts boiled to a pulp and a burnt rice pudding could be passed off as a meal. But there are more of the ones who can cook five things – sausages, sausages, baked beans, hamburgers and sausages – and can't understand why a girl friend with 'flu doesn't seem to want them to cook for her. And even on this side of the Atlantic, we have our share of cute cooks – the ones who are forever handing you out new recipes that always feature six unlikely tins and, all too often, broccoli and canned beetroot and peanut butter as well.

Still, we have far more concerned and interested cooks nowadays who want to know *why* ham on the bone is nicer than flat ham, usually (because the ham trade can take a boneless ham, and bang it around till it takes in several pints of water, that's why). They are interested in *where* the dish came from. They know that eggs cooked in the cream of Normandy, where it rains all the time so the cows are up to their udders in rich grass, will be different from eggs cooked in the olive oil of the Mediterranean, where the cream would go off in half a day, but the olive trees grow on the scraggiest hills. They're prepared to take sides in good old English fights about whether Yorkshire pudding is an individual bun, as we eat it in the effete South, or a great platter of batter cooked under the meat and served before it,

in the (quite hopeless) attempt to take the edge off the Yorkshire appetite.

One day you may become one of these types; one day, you'll either get interested in food or go crazy. But in the meantime, you have to get those characters *fed*. This book is intended to help you through the first frightful fortnight and a bit beyond; to hold your hand while you begin to read better, longer, more committed cookery books. It is not for gourmets – that comes later. It is a lifebelt, not a navigation manual.

The book starts off with a few dead easy recipes to cheer you along. Then there are some kitchen basics and enough down-to-earth know-how to keep you going for a week or two. After that we move into the recipe section proper – and face the possibility that you may be stuck with this thing for some length of time; we consider ways of widening your range and cutting down the work. Finally, you might like to try some variations and take a look at some of the books that you will move on to as you become a real, and no longer just a Temporary/Acting/

Protesting and For-the-Duration-of-the-Emergency cook. After which, dare I say it, with any luck you'll really be enjoying yourself.

SIX EASY RECIPES AND ONE EASY MEAL

The Easiest Main Course in the World
Buy four pieces of chicken. Rub them all over with lots of paprika. Pour a tin of undiluted condensed soup over them (mushroom, say, or celery) and bake at Reg. 4 (350F, 180C) for 1 hour.

The Easiest Roast in the World
Lay the joint on a sheet of foil and shake over it any packet of onion soup. Seal the foil loosely round, and roast according to the times on page 40. When you open it up, the gravy will have made itself.

The Easiest Pudding in the World
For four people, take a small 5 oz pot of double cream; beat it nearly – not quite – stiff. Slice up 3 bananas; break into pieces 3 bought meringues. Mix all together with a dessertspoon of sugar. Make it within an hour or so of eating.

Another version of this uses 6 broken-up ginger biscuits instead of meringue.

The Easiest First Course in the World
Put 2 small Philadelphia Cream Cheeses into a tin of Crosse and Blackwell's consommé with a teaspoon of curry powder and a crushed tooth of garlic and mix or put in blender. Fill small pots with this and put it in the fridge to set.

The **second easiest** is a form of *oeufs en gelée*. Put a piece of pâté about an inch square at the bottom of each little pot; then half a hard-boiled egg; then pour consommé over it and leave to set in fridge.

Warning. Not all brands of consommé set firm so some won't do. And it needs, of course, to keep cool – I once made some for a classy Glyndebourne picnic, and the basket was stowed next to the engine, and it melted all over the chicken legs, the raspberries, the French bread. . . .

The Easiest Cake in the World

1 small pot natural yoghurt

2 of this pot full of self-
 raising flour

1½ pots sugar

¼ pot cooking oil

2 eggs

grated rind of one lemon

pinch of salt

Mix. Bake at Reg. 4 (350F, 180C) for ¾ hour.

The Easiest Pâté in the World

1 lb chicken livers

1 lb sausage meat

¼ lb minced pie veal

¼ lb cooked ham

4 rashers any smoked bacon

2 onions

1 tooth garlic (or more)

2 teaspoons herbs – thyme,
 oregano, parsley,
 marjoram or mixed

Put all this through the mincer. Put it in a casserole and cook at Reg. 3 (325F, 160C) for an hour and a quarter. Cool.

This serves about 10. If you don't want that much, cut up thick slices and freeze them separately, so that they are ready for

* Unexpected people.
* Picnics.
* To use with *oeufs en gelée* (p. 9).

The Easiest Meal in the World

Absolutely fresh bread

A perfect cheese – runny Brie
 or fresh Cheddar or
 Stilton

An enormous Cox's Orange
Pippin or half a pound of
ripe greengages

A glass of red wine

I mention this only because it's possible to get so dogged by this cooking thing that you can forget it doesn't have to be done every single blasted time.

Any meal can be stretched by the addition of noodles to any-thing.

Betty Macdonald

PART TWO

Digging in for the siege

A WEEK'S FAMILY MEALS (all in this book, or bought ready cooked)

Sunday: Roast chicken, peas, roast potatoes; Chocolate Mousse.

Monday: Sausages and chips; packet cheesecake.

Tuesday: Chicken vol-au-vent (buy the cases frozen), mashed potatoes, grilled tomatoes; Blackbirds.

Wednesday: Ham, potato salad, bean shoot and onion salad; Apple Cornflake Bake.

Thursday: Cheesy vegetables; bought steamed pudding.

Friday: Chinese takeaway meal; Choc Ices.

Saturday: Shepherd's Pie; Summer Pudding.

The Next Week of Family Food (though she *swore* she'd be back Friday)

Sunday: Bacon joint roasted with onions, baked potatoes; Liz Ray's Creamy Apple Pudding.

Monday: Beefburgers in buns; fruit yoghurt.

Tuesday: Bacon cakes, peas, mashed potatoes; ice cream and drizzle.

Wednesday: Bought pork pie, potato salad, cole slaw; hot fruit crumble.

Thursday: Piperade, corn fritters; brandy snaps with cream.

Friday: Fish and chips; Angel Delight.

Saturday: Spaghetti Bolognese; Boodle's Oodle Foodle (made with Dream Topping if you're broke).

PLANNING PITFALLS

Oh thou who didst with pitfall and with gin
Beset the path I was to wander in...

Gin, too much of, is not the only pitfall for the aspiring cook. There is also **The Irish Error**. My husband was once offered in Ireland a meal of pork pancake, followed by lentil soup with croûtons, then fish mousse, then a huge stuffed steak and a big fancy ice cream. 'It's this attitude of eat up, boys, we're back to potatoes tomorrow,' he groaned. Don't, because you're trying to impress, make everything too heavy, too fancy, too rich. Only one thing with cream in it; only one fried thing if possible. The idea is to please the digestion, not stun it into submission.

Then there's **Bloxford's Paradox.** Bloxford found that when he planned an excellent casserole, he might vaguely aim to have a first course or a vegetable or a pudding; but was so overcome with how lovely it was going to be that his guests usually just got the casserole, full stop. When, however, he was offering just beefburger, he would add a slight shrimp cocktail, just to cheer things along; and maybe a couple of vegetables, and perhaps better get some salad, and a bought pudding ... He'd end up with a meal twice as complicated and twice as expensive as the swank casserole one. Watch it.

The **Two Time Loser** tries something out, following the recipe exactly – result, success. Second time round, he over-corrects on small faults, takes his eye off the ball – result, failure. It is highly dangerous to serve things for company the *second* time you have them.

And some aim for the **Wrong Audience.** You can sometimes try so hard to show them you can cook, that they end up wishing you'd never learned. You can serve something far too exotic to children – mussels in saffron rice, curried frogs' balls – I will never forget the tears trickling down the face of my seven-year-old, as he looked down at the whitebait and forty tiny eyes looked up at him. Old folk with dodgy digestions, squeamish children, convalescents and country cousins used to a marvellous roast will not thank you if the food's too fancy.

But don't, either, think that **anything you can do I can do better.** Oh, no you can't. Don't try and impress roasting cooks with a roast, a passing Mexican with guacamole. Stick to something *you* know how to do best.

HOW TO READ A RECIPE

Or What the Hell do You Mean, 'Some'?

The trouble with recipes is that either they explain in a told-to-the-children manner exactly what you have to do – in which case they will *look* long and complicated. Or the recipe looks short and simple; but may be highly tricky because it hasn't explained enough. 'To a smooth brown roux', it says laughingly, 'add a pint of stock and some blanched beans ...'

Read a recipe right through before you even decide to tackle it – it may contain a landmine like 'leave for five hours'. Don't be put off by the number of things needed – the pâté on p. 10 and the cake on p. 10 have a lot of things in them, to be sure, but practically all you do is stir: not difficult.

When you try a new recipe, do exactly what it says the first time – then if it tastes lousy, it *is* lousy – it isn't that you've fouled it up. And whenever you make a change in a recipe, make a rough note of it – nothing more infuriating than being unable to repeat some dazzling success.

Here's a list of words that often crop up in recipes:

Stock – the flavoury liquid in which meat or vegetable has cooked. You can use a stock cube but it's not always as good.

Blanch – to plunge vegetables briefly in boiling water.

Scald – to bring, e.g. milk, up to the boil to kill germs.

Baste – spoon fat over a joint as you roast it.

Simmer – bring something to the boil and turn down the heat so that it just barely bubbles.

Fold in – what you do with egg whites you've beaten stiff – you scoop whatever you're mixing them with very gently over them, not stirring – beaten egg whites are a mass of tiny balloons, if you bash them they burst.

Seasoned flour – flour into which you have mixed salt, pepper and probably herbs.

Parboil – part-boil; you often do this to things like carrots before cooking them in the oven.

Brown the meat – means fry, in fat, until outside changes colour – more grey than brown, actually.

Roux – what happens when you melt fat, stir in flour, then add a liquid – same principle as white sauce, p. 15.

Joint the chicken – it sounds easy to cut a chicken into joints; it isn't, even with proper chicken scissors. Buy the pieces ready cut.

Giblets – neck, liver and unmentionable parts of chicken, duck, etc.

Bouquet garni – little bundle of fresh herbs you put in during cooking and fish out at the end. Shove in a teaspoon of Mixed Herbs or Italian Seasoning instead.

Bain Marie – relax – you do not have to bath the au pair girl. It is simply a tin – e.g. a roasting tin – half-filled with water into which you put something that's to cook slowly, like a custard.

MEASUREMENTS

Or Not to Worry

Beginners are always alarmed by the difficulty of knowing how big is a cup (like Anne Scott James' bra sizes – coffee cup, tea cup, champagne cup or Challenge cup). What do they *mean* by a pinch, how big *is* a teaspoon? And I've tried to calm your nerves by spelling out some information in the end covers. But if you watch experienced cooks in action, they don't measure – which is why you needn't panic about it all. We writers can't very well say 'add some onion' or you would rightly scream 'how MUCH onion, for heaven's sake?' but actually it doesn't matter particularly if it's two small ones or one biggish one or two medium ones. One of the reasons (not the only one) that your own cooking is usually more interesting than endless tins and packets is that it doesn't come out the same every time – and the fact that you don't always get the ingredients exactly the same each time is why.

It only matters to get the proportions dead right for baking (baking powder, etc.) or if you are using a strong spice like chilli or curry, or you'll blow the roof of your mouth off. Otherwise, relax. It's something the same with oven temperatures: we all talk as if every stove was identical but it ain't necessarily so – witness Clarence Day's mother, whose two worries were Father and the stove: whenever she gave her full attention to one of them, the other went out. A friend of mine who had cooked on gas all her life has recently gone to live with an Aga; she says she at last realises that all oven times are negotiable – you *can't* switch an Aga up and down at will.

Jack Sprat could eat no fat
His wife could eat no lean –
A real sweet pair of neurotics.
Jack Sharkey

WHAT DO YOU PUT IT IN?

Place in oven at Regulo Whatsit, it says; but it doesn't say what *in*. If you start off a stew or a casserole by browning (frying) the meat or some vegetables, you probably start in the frying pan, then put everything in a crockery pot to put in the oven. If you have one of those heavy iron pots with an iron handle, you can do the whole job in one – and bring it to table in it too: saves washing-up. Only meat loaf, cake or bread needs a tin. If you're doing a tart or a flan, a tin with a removable bottom makes it easier to get the rim off and cut the tart.

For anything that sticks badly, like scrambled egg or hot milk, use a non-stick saucepan if you've got one. If you're starting from scratch on the casserole/vegetable dish front, get a set of white soufflé dishes – they'll do for everything, including puddings. Anything which has a pastry top has to have a lip or running-board round the rim: wet it first.

A FEW BASICS YOU MIGHT AS WELL LEARN

Grilling and Frying
This always seems the easy option; unfortunately you do need rather good meat. To fry, use if possible a mixture of butter and oil – butter alone is more apt to burn. To grill, wipe the meat with oil and heat the grill first. The times are much the same: **Lamb Chops:** For brown outside, pink within – 4 minutes each side. For well done – 8 minutes each side (if chops an inch thick, add an extra minute). **Steaks:** As for chops. To fry them, use the minimum of fat and get the pan very hot. It's *very* hard to get a 'well done' steak really tender. **Veal and Pork Chops:** Don't have the heat as high as it will go; cook on medium heat for 10 minutes a side. **Veal Escalopes:** Beaten flat, 2 minutes a side, medium heat.

White Sauce
This is the basic principle for cheese sauce, sauce for casseroles and many others, so it's worth mastering.

Melt 2 oz butter over low heat in saucepan. Add 2 oz flour and stir it in till all is absorbed – looks very dry at this stage. Then slowly add $\frac{1}{2}$ pint milk (for a thick sauce) and stir for 5 minutes till flour thickens. If it gets lumps, stir like mad and stop adding liquid till you've got the lumps out – easier to press them out against side of the pan when sauce is thick. Now add $\frac{1}{2}$ teaspoon salt, a couple of turns of pepper mill and any flavourings you're using, e.g. grated cheese. Make sure it cooks for at least 10 minutes in total or it will taste floury.

Coffee
The world is full of cute machines for making coffee, but you can do perfectly well by putting a tablespoonful of coffee for

each large cup into a jug, and pouring on the water. Leave for a few minutes, then strain into the cups. If you've no strainer, put an eggcupful of *cold* water in to settle the grounds, and pour out carefully.

Rice
Some deep-rooted fear of the mysterious east must be what makes otherwise carefree people scared of rice. These two ways are dead easy; or you can buy a packet of Uncle Ben and follow the instructions on the packet. There are dozens of types and methods, but I always use long-grain.

Method 1. Put on a *big* pan of water to boil; when boiling put in a teaspoonful of salt and the rice, allowing 2 oz (2 rounded tablespoons) per person. Boil away hard for 12 minutes, as the grains must be kept on the move or they'll stick together. Then test – *if a grain pressed against a hard surface has no hard white dot in the middle, it's done*. Drain off the water (if it still seems on the wet side, you can put it in a low oven (Reg. $\frac{1}{2}$–2, 240F–300F, 120C–150C) for a few minutes; but it's not usually necessary).

Method 2. Absolutely foolproof. Put on a kettle to heat. Meanwhile measure your rice (2 oz or 2 rounded tablespoons per person) into a jug. Then melt 2 dessertspoons of oil, or oil-and-butter, in a pan with a lid, and fry your rice for a couple of minutes. Then add exactly twice as much liquid as you had rice – that's why you had to measure it in the jug. Add 1 teaspoon salt and any herbs or colourings (e.g. a teaspoon of turmeric per cup of rice turns it a pleasant yellow). Clamp the lid on with a tea-towel between lid and pan and set over lowest possible heat for $\frac{1}{2}$ hour. Then turn it off; it will keep warm if necessary for at least another 10 minutes.

Pancakes

1 egg	$\frac{1}{2}$ pint milk
4 oz flour	$\frac{1}{2}$ teaspoon salt

Mix till your arm aches; leave for an hour if you can (but it's not fatal if you can't). Heat a frying pan (non-stick for choice) for a minute or two over medium flame; then add a teaspoon or so of oil. Pour in enough mixture just to reach towards edge of pan. Wait till edges begin to look firm, and it's golden brown underneath when you lift it. Turn over with fish slice; wait till that side is browny coloured and move to hot plate in very low oven.

The old saying says: 'the first pancake is never the best.' Actually in my case the first pancake is rarely even edible; so make

---

Eat, drink and be merry
for tomorrow ye diet.

Lewis C. Henry

---

enough batter to allow for this – e.g. double the above quantities if you're 6.

Pastry

8 oz flour	¼ teaspoon salt
4 oz butter or marge or lard	3 tablespoons water
or a mixture of these	(1 tablespoon sugar)

Rub the fat into the flour with the tips of your fingers till it looks like fine breadcrumbs. Then add a tablespoon of sugar if it's for a fruit pie. Add the water, mix and gather into a ball with minimum manhandling. Liberally flour a board or flat surface and the rolling pin (or bottle if you haven't one). Roll it out first in one direction, then the other; and cut out your flan/pie-top or whatever. Bake at Reg. 5 (375F, 190C) for 15 minutes, or more if whatever is in your pie requires longer – move a fruit pie lower in the oven, for example, to cook the fruit.

Mayonnaise

Put 1 egg yolk into a big bowl, add ½ teaspoon French mustard. Put ¼ pint olive oil in a little jug, and very carefully dribble it into the yolk, stirring hard; it has to be almost drop by drop at first. When all oil is used up, add 1 dessertspoon vinegar, ¼ teaspoon salt, 2 turns pepper mill.

If it curdles, *either* drop an ice cube in, which ought to bring it back to its OK gluey state; or liberate another yolk and dribble your failed sauce even more slowly into it.

But for sauce tartare, seafood sauce, sandwiches, etc. use Hellmann's or Bennett's – they're not the same but they're pretty good.

French Dressing

2 tablespoons oil (preferably olive)	¼ teaspoon salt
	2 turns pepper mill
1 tablespoon vinegar (preferably wine)	½ teaspoon French mustard

Mix in bottom of salad bowl; or, better still, make up a whole lot – ½ pint oil, ¼ pint vinegar, etc. – and keep in an old Chianti bottle (the straw catches the drips) giving it an almighty shake each time. Use less vinegar if you prefer it bland.

All-Purpose Brown Sauce (low-class, but useful)

Fry 1 finely-chopped onion in 1 dessertspoon oil or butter for 5 minutes. Mix 2 dessertspoons Bisto or gravy powder with 1 cup water and add. Then add 2 tablespoons tomato purée (½ a tin), 2 turns of pepper mill, and cook for 5 minutes.

Note. Don't add salt till you've tasted it; the gravy powder has some.

Good for meatballs (with noodles), for heating up scraps of leftover beef, or for pouring over any bright idea you may have had which is coming out too dry. Hide it from your Cordon Bleu friends.

HOW DO YOU . . . ?

Separate an egg yolk from its white? Break the egg cleanly in two, holding the yolk in one half as the white dribbles down into (we hope) a bowl you've put underneath. Pass the egg yolk carefully from one half to the other till all the egg white is drained off.

Measure a flat spoonful? Scrape it off flat with a knife.

Chop herbs? Take a knife that has a straight, not curved, cutting edge; hold down the point and bang the blade up and down by the handle onto the herbs.

Whisk egg white? If you haven't got a whisk, you get on quicker whisking with a knife on a plate than with a fork in a bowl. Don't ask me why.

Clean leeks? You have to slit them down the side, usually; they get filth in their very innermost being.

Wash lettuce? If you've no shaker, run each leaf under the tap, put it in a tea towel and whirl it round your head. Being careful to hold onto the ends – my son didn't, once, and found it very embarrassing saying over the garden wall, 'please can we have our salad back?' Actually winter lettuces, grown under glass, usually don't need washing at all.

Make breadcrumbs? First dry the crusts or bread in a low oven until hard. Then put between two bits of newspaper (or tea towels) and bash with rolling pin or empty bottle until all is crumbled. Keep in a screwtop jar.

WHAT TO DO WITH A . . .

Leftover Yolk
It will keep in the fridge for a day or two if you cover it (un-broken) with cold water. Use for mayonnaise, or include in scrambled eggs; or thicken a casserole.

Leftover White
Make a whisky sour, of course. As follows:

1 white of egg	1 dessertspoon sugar (or 3
1 lemon	saccharine)
	3 bottle caps whisky

Mix sugar or saccharine in the juice of the lemon before you add anything else. Then put in egg white and whisky and whisk briefly.

But what if I have *two* egg whites? Well, that's it, of course – when it comes to whiskies sour, once is *not* enough: make another.

The whites, I suppose I have to tell you, keep for days and days in the fridge, and you could tip them into scrambled egg or make meringue.

KEEPING IT FRESH

Uncooked meat will keep for 4 days in a refrigerator, mince 3 days and 'offal' – e.g. liver – much less, 2 days at most. A cooked casserole or remains of a joint may last up to a week *if* you get it into the fridge as soon as it's cool; let it sit around a warm kitchen all night and you've lost 2 days.

If you've no fridge, **marinade** your meat – even if you have a fridge, it makes it more tender. Make up some French dressing, p. 17; cut up the meat and cover with dressing; add a chopped-up onion, and a bay leaf if you have one. That'll keep 2 days in hot weather, 3 in winter.

Keep **butter** cool by wrapping it in paper and putting a flower pot over it and keeping all this wet – it's the evaporating water that takes heat from the butter. Similarly, **wine** can be chilled by wrapping wet newspaper round it. If you're reading this in a hot holiday cottage with no fridge, you'd probably better boil the milk – doesn't taste too good, but nor does sour milk.

HOW MUCH DO I NEED?

Meat: Allow ¼ lb per person. Obviously, you may need a bit more if the meat's presented alone – as mince, say – than if it's mixed with a million vegetables in a casserole.

Potatoes: Allow ½ lb per person; rather less if you're cooking for a lot of people, as slimmers ye have always with you.

Green vegetables: You can get away with ¼ lb per person of something like green beans; fresh peas, where you chuck out the pod, allow ½ lb.

Chicken: A 4 lb chicken will make 2 meals for 4 people. How much they eat first time round decides what you make for the second time.

Wine: The old adage used to be – one bottle between 2 generous; one between 3, pour carefully; one between 4, not enough. If there are 4 of you, get a litre bottle – better value anyway.

HOW DO I KNOW WHEN . . . ?

The deep fat's hot enough to fry? When a small bit of bread dropped into it browns in not more than a minute.

The shallow fat's hot enough to fry? When a very faint haze begins to rise from it.

The oven's hot enough? 'Pre-heating' never takes more than 12 minutes; for a medium or low oven, 7 or 5 will do. If it's a slow-cooking thing like a casserole, don't bother.

The onions are cooking at the right temperature? They hiss faintly, like contented snakes.

The spaghetti is cooked? Press a strand against a hard surface and see if there's a thread of starch still uncooked; if not, it's done.

Cake is cooked? Stick in a skewer or a knitting needle; when it comes out clean, you're there.

Potatoes, sprouts are cooked? When a fork goes easily right into them.

A roast chicken is cooked? When a spike pressed in near the leg goes in very easily and no blood or pinkish liquid oozes from the hole.

Roast meat is done? When a carving fork goes in easily, no blood oozes – but stick to the times in the roasting table on p. 44.

The meat's gone off? Smell is your best guide – and if something's been in the fridge, leave it out for half an hour because the cold may have held in the smell. Or offer it to a cat – if the cat does eat it, it's OK though the converse, alas, is not true – cats are so darned fussy.

20

PART THREE

Twenty simple recipes for filling them up

EGGS AND BREAKFASTS

'She can't even boil an egg' used to be the thing they said about
duchesses and/or the gadabout girls their sons were threatening
to marry. But all these simple breakfast things can be done better
or worse.

Boiled Eggs
You were taught $3\frac{1}{2}$ minutes – but that was before fridges. A
fridge-cold egg needs $4\frac{1}{2}$ minutes after it goes into a pan of boiling
water. Hard boiled is 10 minutes.

Scrambled Eggs
These need the old French instructions: plenty of butter, plenty
of time. To make scrambled eggs for 2 take 4 (yes, 4) eggs; beat
them for a minute in a bowl; melt a heaped teaspoonful of butter
in a saucepan, tip in eggs and stir over very low heat. Add a
teaspoon salt, and 2 turns of the pepper mill. Stop just *before*
they seem hard enough. *Don't* add milk; *don't* turn up the heat
to hurry them up – that's how school scrambled eggs got so
nasty.

Bacon and Eggs
Bacon can cook fast but eggs should start at a low heat or you
get that bit of crinkled plastic at the back. So in a perfect world,
you grill the bacon and fry the eggs very slowly in some bacon
fat which you already have. Otherwise, cook the bacon, heave
it out on to kitchen paper to drain, turn the heat way down and
carefully break in the eggs, putting the bacon back in the pan

for a few seconds at the end to re-heat. If there's jelly-wobble on eggs that are otherwise perfect, spoon some of the fat over them to finish them off.

Poached Eggs
Heat salted water to boiling in a wide pan (or frying pan). Break the eggs in and immediately turn heat down. Minimum cooking time is about 3 minutes; they can sit in the water with heat off till you need them.

Omelettes
Break 2 eggs into a bowl, add a pinch of salt and a turn of pepper mill; beat lightly. Heat a small, preferably non-stick pan over a medium high flame. Put in a small nut of butter, or marge, or a spoonful of oil. When there's a very faint haze coming off the fat, pour them in. After a second or two, push the egg away from the side to let more touch the hot part of the pan. If there's a filling, add it now. Then fold over the omelette and hoosh it on to a plate. What you want is *assez baveuse* – dribbly. The eggs should only be in the pan for less than a minute.

Good Fillings
grated cheese
fried mushrooms (6 minutes in separate pan)

2 onions and 2 tomatoes fried (with or without a dash of curry powder)
chopped ham (can be mixed with eggs from the start)

See also **Piperade, Portuguese Eggs**, p. 24.

BASIC SLAG
or Don't Tell Elizabeth David

Mince is usually about the cheapest easy meat going. This basic mixture can be doctored in several different ways.

Basic Mixture: *Per 1 lb mince*
2 onions (3 if you're feeling extra hard up)
2 dessertspoons oil
1 dessertspoon tomato paste
1 crushed tooth garlic

2 heaped tablespoons flour
mixed herbs
¼ teaspoon ground cloves
½ teaspoon salt
pepper

Chop onions finely, fry in oil over medium heat for 5 minutes. Then add mince, bodging it around until all the red is gone. Mix in the flour. Add one large cup water and all seasonings.

Put this in Reg. 3 (325F, 160C) for 2 hours. For **Mince** add a teaspoonful of Marmite or Bovril and just one lidful of gravy browning.

For **Shepherd's Pie,** proceed as for mince, meanwhile boiling and mashing 1 lb of potatoes. Put mince in a pie dish; if it looks a bit dry, add another cupful of water. Then spread mashed potato over the top, put a few little bits of butter on it and cook at Reg. 5 (375F, 190C) for 20 minutes.

For **Spaghetti Sauce** add 1 tin of tomatoes and 1 5-oz tin of tomato purée (and preferably a teaspoon of oregano or basil).

For **Chilli con Carne** as for spaghetti but add ¼ teaspoon chilli powder (more if you like it, but *taste first*) and 2 tins of baked beans with their sauce washed off under a tap.

For **Moussaka** slice up an aubergine and fry in more oil than you would think they need – you keep having to add more. Then put mince and aubergine in alternate layers in a casserole. Make a pint of white sauce with 1 oz butter, 1 oz flour and 1 pint milk; beat in another bowl 2 eggs and add to the sauce. Pour this over the dish, sprinkle with 2 tablespoons grated cheese and cook at Reg. 5 (375F, 190C) for ¾ hour.

SIMPLE SUPPERS

Kippers
Put one kipper for each person in a jug; pour boiling water on them and leave for 10 minutes. (Frying is marginally nicer – about 4 minutes a side – but the smell is awful.) Serve with brown bread and butter.

Easy Cheesy Vegetables
Gather up all the oddments of vegetables you've got – fresh or frozen; it really doesn't matter which ones, though a bit of onion helps. Put on a pan of salted water; chop up the vegetables and keep each kind separate, so that you add the ones that cook slowest first. Put in about a handful of each in this order: *first*, any onion, celery, carrot, green pepper; *second*, green beans, mushrooms, cauliflower, courgettes; *last*, tomatoes, frozen peas, bean shoots or shreds of Chinese leaf.

While this is going on make a cheese sauce, melting 1 tablespoon butter, blending in 2 tablespoons flour and adding ¾ pint milk (as on p. 15); when it's cooked for about 7 minutes stir in 4 oz grated cheese, salt and pepper. Drain the vegetables and pour the sauce over them.

Cauliflower Cheese
This is of course exactly the same, except that you have only cauliflower; add a teaspoon of mustard to the sauce, and put it under the grill for a few minutes to get brown.

Croque Monsieur
For each person, cut the crusts off two slices of bread; make a sandwich with a slice of ham and a slice (or bits) of cheese (ideally Gruyère) and fry until golden brown both sides. Serve with grilled tomatoes.

Welsh Rarebit   *For 4*
3 tablespoons milk	2 egg yolks
½ lb cheese, grated	salt, pepper, Worcester Sauce

Warm milk, gradually stir in the grated cheese until all is melted. Then add the egg yolks (they stop it all separating out, as so often can happen). Stir for a minute, then pour it over the toast; which you've put on some flat dish that will go under the grill. Brown it briefly under the grill.

This is also marvellous on *warm crumpets* instead of toast.

Piperade   *For 4*

2 onions	6 eggs
2 green peppers	salt, pepper
4 tomatoes	½ teaspoon oregano or basil
1 crushed tooth garlic	

Chop up the vegetables and fry gently till they are soft – about 15 minutes. Add salt, pepper, herbs, garlic. Then simply break the eggs into the frying pan and stir them around. Stop when there are no transparent bits of the white, but all is still soft.

Portuguese Eggs
('Portuguese' is the word you use for anything with tomato in it that you can't get away with calling 'Provençale'.)

6 eggs	2 oz butter
6 tomatoes	2 oz flour
1 tooth garlic (important)	⅔ pint milk
1 tablespoon parsley	3 oz cheese, grated
(optional)	salt, pepper
1 teaspoon oregano or basil	

Hard-boil the eggs, cool them enough to chop them in slices. Skin the tomatoes and fry them for just a minute or two with the garlic and the herbs. Put them in the bottom of a shallow dish, lay the sliced eggs on top, sprinkle with chopped parsley if you're using it.

Now make a sauce by melting the butter, blending in the flour, gradually adding the milk and finally the grated cheese; cook for 5 more minutes. Pour it over the eggs and put the whole dish under the grill for 3 minutes.

This also makes an excellent first course for 8.

Any mother should be able to cook just ordinary English food – you know, spaghetti, ravioli, macaroni …

Jasper Conran

PADDING

Garlic Bread
Take a torpedo-shaped French loaf and cut nearly all the way through as if for thick slices. Pound 2 teeth of garlic with 1 oz (or more according to the size of the loaf) of butter; spread this down each cut. Put in low oven Reg. 2 (300F, 150C) for about 10 minutes, and if someone comes to the door later, remember not to give them a big kiss.

Chips

Cut up chips from big potatoes and if possible leave them with salt over them for at least ¼ hour, then dry them. Heat deep fat (it's ready when a cube of bread browns in a minute or less). Put in chips and cook till just underdone – still yellow, not brown. Lift them out and drain. Re-heat fat between each batch. Put them back to finish off *just* before you eat them; drain on kitchen-paper or newspaper.

Corn Fritters   *For 4–6*

5 oz flour	1 tablespoon melted fat
3 teaspoons baking powder	6 tablespoons milk
1 teaspoon salt	1 small tin sweetcorn
1 teaspoon sugar	oil for frying
2 eggs	

Mix dry ingredients, then drain sweetcorn. Then mix everything together thoroughly. Drop in dollops into shallow fat, frying about 4 minutes each side – till golden brown. This amount makes 8 fritters.

MYTHS

You have to scald milk before using it in puddings
To stop it going off and ruining your pudding. Now that just about all milk is pasteurised, it won't.

You must never re-freeze meat
Yes, you can; this myth is a hangover from the early tremulous days of freezing and related to shopkeepers not trying to re-freeze packeted stuff in their display cabinets. If you thaw and re-freeze things several times, the colour and taste maybe won't be absolutely as good, but the bacteria are stopped in their tracks by the freezing process anyway – provided you have a 3-star freezing compartment.

You have to blanch all vegetables before freezing
Not so. Blanching kills enzymes, which affect taste and colour; not bacteria, which are what do you harm. Many people prefer crisper veg. that is less green; if you're not freezing for more than a week or two none of it matters anyway.

You mustn't put cheese in the fridge
Depends on the cheese. It won't hurt mousetrap, what could? It's kept in refrigeration before it got to you anyway. It's things like Brie which are ruined by the cold.

DISASTERS (now here I really *am* an expert)

Chip-pan on fire
Resist the urge to throw water on it (which will spray burning fat all over the room) or rush with it to the window/sink/fire station. Throw a cloth over it – a burned cloth costs a lot less than a burned house.

Too much salt/chilli/curry powder
A lump of butter may do the trick – depends how much too much. A raw potato added can also help. Otherwise, you have to add more of something else to spread the spice among more food – which is how I came to invent that excellent dish Chilli con Spinach.

Casserole too runny
You can thicken it nearly instantly three ways:

1. Mix a tablespoon of cornflour in a cup with a little of the slosh, then stir it in for a few minutes.
2. Ditto with a couple of egg yolks – don't let it boil after that.
3. Sprinkle instant mashed potato, the powder, not the chunks.

Why not flour? Because that has to cook for about 10 minutes, or there is a strong taste of wallpaper paste.

Blocked sink
Very effective is the black rubber sucker on the end of a stick that plumbers use – but buy the *big* one, the little one's not much good. A mixture of washing soda and boiling water is supposed to clear a sink, and sometimes even does.

You've dropped it
When the food goes on the floor in front of the people who were going to eat it, you need the aplomb of the woman whose maid dropped the turkey as it was being served. Everyone knew they were going to eat it anyway, but it seemed scarcely polite just to hoick it back on to the dish … 'Take it away, Mary,' said the hostess calmly. 'And bring in the other one.'

Burnt food
When something has burned and stuck to the pan, *don't scrape.* Tip out into another pan everything that will come without scraping. You'll have less, of course, but what's left, with any luck, won't taste of the burnt bits, still safely stuck to the pan. By the same token, when you scrape *burnt toast*, tap it, burnt side downwards, over the sink – and don't butter it with the same knife you've scraped it with.

Oven has not turned on
If it's gas, don't belatedly try and light it – I have a friend who lost half her hair in such an explosion. Open the oven door, flap it back and forth and wait 10 minutes before you even try to light it. If it's electric, check the fuse in the plug – and that you did actually remember to turn it on.

Feeling shivery, a cold coming on
Vin chaude à l'orange is the most comforting thing alive: put a large cupful of red wine in a saucepan with a lump of sugar, a twist of orange peel, a pinch of clove (or 2 cloves) a pinch of cinnamon; heat just to boiling point. It may not cure you, but you won't care, anyway. OR make a **toddy** with 2 parts whisky, 1 part orange squash and 4 parts boiling water, with cloves, cinnamon, sugar as above. If you're making this for a child, leave out the whisky; an eggcupful of Ginger Wine (if you have it) puts the little one firmly to sleep.

Feeling sick
Children, or even people, who are feeling sick should be kept off anything fatty, and re-cooked sugar (like jam); anything scrunchy like salads, or hard to absorb, like meat. Stick to fruit juice, soup, bland things like bread, purées, poached eggs on mashed potatoes, Marmite-on-toast, soda water, tea. If someone is actually vomiting, a grated apple *with the skin on* often stops it.

Red wine down her dress
Immediately rub in a lot of salt; brush out later.

Fat down his suit
Immediately rub in flour or talcum powder; brush out later.

Coffee, tea, soup or indeed almost anything else spilt over clothes
Immediately run it with cold water; better still, take it off and soak it (you've the basis of an interesting evening there).

Broken china
You can stick almost anything with Araldite if you've the patience. Don't use minor glues for major jobs or you'll meet the disaster of my father, when a teacup handle came unstuck and his boiling tea poured into his lap.

You've run out of bread
Right. Make a loaf of soda bread in the Irish manner. As follows:

Soda Bread
1 lb flour	$\frac{1}{2}$ pint sour milk (or ordinary
1 teaspoon salt	milk with a spoonful of
1 teaspoon bicarbonate of soda	vinegar added)

Mix dry things; turn on oven at Reg. 6 (400F, 200C). Add the sour milk – if it's too stiff to handle add a bit more – some flours mop up more than others. Grease a flat tin and plop the stuff on it; bake for 45 minutes. Leave till cool before cutting.

PART FOUR

Digging in for the longer term

PLANNING WHAT TO EAT

Making up the menu is one of the hardest things about cooking and I'm so woefully bad at it that I'm always planning chicken soup followed by chicken, or melon for first course and a fruit pudding; or giving them mince one day and shepherd's pie the next.

One way out is to think of foods in categories, and not pick two from any one category in the same week.

Sunday: 1. Swank. A roast; or beef olives; or veal; or pork kebabs; or something that takes a serious piece of meat.

Monday: 2. Joe's Caff. Sausages and mash; fish and chips; beans on toast; beefburgers in buns; or any of those Brunchies, Cheesies, Scroungies and Junkies they sell from the freezer.

Tuesday: 3. Leftover Day. Rice dishes; or a British curry; or rissoles; or chicken fricassee: or a general round-up of whatever is in the fridge and will soon go off.

Wednesday: 4. Something Cold. With soup if it's winter. Corned beef and cole slaw; ham with tomatoes and apple-and-celery; a bought pie with potato salad and cucumber; those cheap tongues you get in vacuum packs with bean shoots and onions.

Thursday: 5. Gunge. A pot of beans and bacon; cauliflower cheese; macaroni cheese; an egg dish; cheesy vegetables; Pro-vençale potatoes.

Friday: 6. Something Different. If you can't get yourself taken out, get something from the Chinese takeaway or a takeaway pizza or make one of the others cook or try something new and alarming.

Saturday: 7. Family Standby. Spaghetti; lasagne; corned beef hash; shepherd's pie; stew; chicken casserole; 'a goloptious full-up potful'.

CUTTING DOWN THE WORK

Washing up. Everybody hates it, yet most people do almost nothing to make it less tiresome; I often think the British attitude to washing up has far more to do with the national masochism and Letting You Know How I Suffer than actually getting any-thing clean.

First, let pans soak – overnight if need be. In the morning you won't have to scrape at them at all, and it's better for the pans as well as your temper. If you can't bear to leave pans soaking, you won't have trouble surviving in the kitchen – you'll have trouble surviving anywhere else.

Second, **don't dry**. Get a proper plate rack – I mean one that will hold everything you use, including the cutlery, and leave every single thing to dry itself at least once. Then you will find that amazingly little needs drying at all – glasses don't, for example, if they've been rinsed in hot water. If you are genuinely distressed by the sight of drying plates, do what they do in Scandinavia – have **a plate-rack in a bottomless cupboard** over the draining-board. Then you can shut the doors on the dishes and they go on drying behind.

And if there are four or more of you, start saving now for a **dishwasher**. I've heard hundreds of reasons why they're supposed to be a waste of money – but only once from someone who's actually had one; and she only gave up because she'd a fleet of teenagers to wash up for her. Some of us find motivating teenagers even harder work than washing up.

You have a better hope of **getting other people to do things** for themselves if they know where everything is – label it if necessary. Think of the sort of husband who can't boil his wife an egg on her birthday without calling up the stair eighteen times, 'Where's the pan, darling . . . where's the salt . . . darling, can you tell me where . . .'

You can avoid washing umpteen serving dishes by using oven-to-tableware – metal pots that will also go on the top of the stove are best of all. Use paper plates and napkins if the hordes of Midion are descending on you, and get out of the filthy job of emptying the teapot by using teabags, now that even classy teas come in bags. And if the inside of the pot – or a decanter, or a flower-vase – is all gunged up, don't scrub – soak it for an hour in Steradent, the stuff they make for false teeth.

Some **machines** save work; but not all. A waste-disposal unit makes sense in a high flat where they collect the rubbish once a week; not if you've a dustbin outside the back door a yard away, since you have to sort out the things the touchy object won't eat. I prefer a couple of straight-sided bins that live in the cupboard under the sink: then you line them up under work surface or sink edge, and just heave everything over into them.

Avoid **floors** that demand to be washed twice a day, like Betty Macdonald's white pine: 'a substance that just might have been more trouble would have been white velvet'. Beautiful dark floors, too, show dirt hideously, and unimpressive composition tiles hide the gunk far better. Years ago Dennis Wheatley suggested that you build up a patina on your floor: 'Do all your cooking in a pair of felt slippers, if you see what I mean, and don't pick up anything you drop.' I can't say I've tried it. If you have a big eating-kitchen and only the cooking corner gets dirty, cover the rest with an old rug; then you won't feel obliged to wash all of it every time.

WHAT ABOUT GADGETS?

The **equipment** I would struggle quite hard not to be made to cook without includes the following:

A **pinger** (or ringer). You are *always* doing two things at once when you're cooking; it's no good hoping you'll look at your watch and remember when to take the eggs off, or the rice, or how long the beans have been at it.

The kind of **cheese-grater** you can hold over the pan (say) and turn a handle: as illustrated.

The lighter type of **potato-peeler** – makes a really quick job of it.

Flour-blender, if you regularly make gravy: it saves all the anguish of trying to stir out the lumps when you put the flour into the roasting tin (as illustrated).

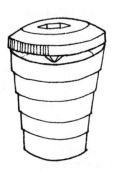

A **garlic-squeezer** if you like garlic at all – the kind with a swinging pusher is better than the kind like a tiny potato-masher.

You need one or two **knives** sharper than the one you have already, another **measuring jug** since the first is in the fridge full of something else, and **more than one frying pan**; somehow people know they need several saucepans but get it wrong about frying pans, which sometimes need to be enormous (for bacon and eggs for six) and sometimes tiny (for frying 1 onion or 1 mushroom); you almost never need the middling tiddler you just hopefully bought at Woolworth's.

Above all, get a **blender** (or liquidiser, as a few still misleadingly call it). With it, you can make soups from anything, crush nuts and ice, make batter, milk-shakes, cocktails; you can pulp fruit, grate cheese, make breadcrumbs and whirl the lumps out of a sauce. You can get one for under ten quid nowadays so the suggestion isn't outrageous; and washing it does *not* make it more trouble than it's worth – it becomes its own little dish-washer and washes itself.

Do you need a pressure cooker? No, not unless you also need ham on the upstairs lampshades. At least that's what my most efficient cousin got when one blew up in her (downstairs) kitchen. A timer on your oven is a better bet if you have to have things ready as soon as you're home from work.

DO YOU NEED A FREEZER?

There are two quite different ways of dealing with a freezer or a big freezing compartment: Good Little Farmwife and Oh, God, dinner. Good Little Farmwife has never really got over the fact that they've invented tins, so her home bottling is not what keeps the family alive during the long winter. However, the chance of spending a fine summer's day indoors chopping and blanching pounds and pounds of runner beans puts the roses back in her cheeks, and if she can also buy half a sheep off some itinerant shepherd (with his own freezer van) she's happy.

There is no need to act like this. The Oh, God, dinner people use their freezers quite differently – simply to freeze the leftovers so they don't have to have it again next day, to make up double quantities of a casserole (not much more trouble) and freeze half of it; to buy a week's supply of frozen juice at a time; to freeze their own labour so that they needn't spend every moment of a holiday weekend cooking; or to cook six things at once, in peace, at the weekend, and then not to have to start from scratch on a busy weekday.

The only trouble is that the Oh, God, dinner people have put off even *thinking* about a meal till the last moment, so they have a terrible time getting things de-frozen in time. However, you

* Put anything that's to be served hot into a very low oven.
* As soon as you can get a knife into it, slice it up, to let the air get at it better.
* Put anything like sausages or fish (in its paper) into lukewarm water (or even hot if you're really pushed).
* Put frozen concentrated orange juice with the right amount of water in the blender – makes it fluffy, kids like that.

BOOKS

There are thousands of cookery books around; I can only suggest a few that I *know* are good, and won't let you down.

Good Housekeeping Encyclopaedia (National Magazine Company). Everyone needs one basic reference book; this has all the standard things very clearly explained – and the individual recipes work.

ABC of Cookery (HM Stationery Office). The Ministry mercifully assumes that you know *nothing*; this tells you all the things the other books assume you know.

French Country Cooking and **Mediterranean Food** by Elizabeth David (Penguin). All books by Elizabeth David not only tell you how to cook, but actually make you want to do it. These two were written at the beginning of her cookery career, before she became quite as scholarly as she is now; so you might perhaps start with them.

Ten Minute Cooking by Edward Pomiane (Faber). For fussy bachelors – I don't think he knows what children *are* – but he keeps the good principles of French cooking even during his ten-minute flap.

The Resourceful Cook by Elizabeth Ray (Macmillan). Whatever she recommends, works. I can't say fairer than that.

For Greek food, Joyce Stubbs' **The Home Book of Greek Cookery** (Faber and paperback) is a bible.

Anything by **Delia Smith** is mouth-watering.

Jocasta Innes' **Pauper's Cookbook** (Penguin) makes being poor a privilege. The information's all there – just pick up a paperback and browse.

If you are greedy and can read – you can cook
Francesca Bredin and about 10,000 others.

THINGS THAT MAKE COOKING FUN
Having plenty of time to shop for what you're going to cook.
Reading Elizabeth David's books.
A warm kitchen with a radio.
A drink while you do it.
Developing a speciality – Chinese cooking, or baking, or even some daft-like thing such as Macrobiotics.
A talkative, appreciative, greedy pig to cook for.

THINGS THAT MAKE COOKING GRIM

Having to watch every last penny of the cost.

Starting when you're tired after work.

Men who can't stand onions.

Children who pick out each separate scrap of mushroom or whine 'I don't like that' before they've tried it.

People who stand one yard away and say, 'I just want to see how you do that' – especially if you're not sure how.

Cooking for people too dumb to realise that cooking is usually only as good as its audience, and who therefore don't say, 'Gee, that's great.'

Eating in front of the television – except occasionally, as a wicked treat.

All sentences beginning, 'What my mother used to do was ...'

What do you do if

they all decide they're going to the pictures and must leave in 20 minutes, can they have lunch first?

Menu for 4

Cheese-and-tomato Eggs

Jelly

Put on a kettle for the jelly, and a big pan ¼ full of salted water for the 8 eggs. Split 4 buns or muffins or baps or make 8 slices of toast; put in a very low oven to keep warm.

Poach eggs in boiling water (3 minutes) and turn off heat; they'll keep warm in their water.

Mix together 4 oz grated cheese, 1 tin tomatoes; mix 1 tablespoon cornflour with a little of the tomato juice; add ½ teaspoon salt, pepper. Stir over a low heat.

Now make up jelly with only *half* a pint of boiling water; when it's dissolved, add ice cubes for the other half; it sets instantly.

Put an egg on each half bun, pour over the cheese–tomato sauce and serve.

Give them their jelly, boot them out the door and settle down for a peaceful afternoon.

PART FIVE

Basic meals and basic courses

SOUP

Soup is the all-purpose comforter; but between a cheap packet and a lobster bisque there are light years of difference.

Many tinned soups, and one or two packets, are good. Brands that we like include: Campbell's Pea and Ham; Heinz Chicken; Baxter's Game (good enough to pass off as your own), almost anything made by Liebig, if you can get them. Batchelor's Cup-o-Soup, especially chicken; Crosse and Blackwell's consomme.

All these are OK as they are, but you can always tart them up a bit.

Try
* Chopped parsley, or chopped chives or spring onion tops or indeed almost anything that's green except the houseplants, sprinkled on each plateful at the last moment.
* Croûtons – made by toasting two slices of bread, cutting into small squares and frying quickly in oil – watch it, they burn fast. Leftover croûtons can be kept in the fridge and reheated.
* A little curry powder in Heinz lentil soup does wonders for it. Likewise a pinch of chilli in any otherwise boring vegetable soup. How much? Start with a quarter teaspoon, and taste as you go.

If you've got a blender you can make soup out of almost anything from a cauliflower to your grandmother's bootlaces – or even your grandmother; **Fridge Soup,** my standby, consists simply of putting all the leftovers in the blender with water and heating up the result. However, they do complain that it sometimes tastes of 'too much and nothing'; if that's the way it's come out, add Marmite or Bovril; or a big squeeze from a tube of tomato purée. Fridge soup seems to stand a better chance of success if there was a bit of bacon or salami among the founding ingredients.

But proper soup, i.e. something you actually intended to be soup from the beginning, is not difficult.

Leek and Potato Soup   *For 4*

3 leeks	top of the milk
2 potatoes	1 pint water (or chicken
butter	stock)

If you have no blender chop leeks and potatoes quite small, as we don't want any nonsense about putting them through a sieve. Fry these in a teaspoon of butter for about 4 minutes, then pour in a pint of hot water; add salt and pepper and let it all simmer for 20 minutes. Add 2 tablespoons top of the milk at the last minute. If you want to blend it into a smooth purée, this is the moment; throw a cloth over the blender to stop it slurping out of the top. We usually blend about half of it, leaving some chunks.

Onion Soup

For each person:

1 onion	butter
1 slice bread	salt
1 oz cheese	pepper

Chop onions finely, fry for 5 minutes in butter in a big pan; add a large cupful of water per onion, plus salt, pepper; simmer ½ hour.

Meanwhile, cut the crusts off the bread, toast it, grate the cheese and pile it on the bread and grill till cheese melts. Pour soup into bowls, and float one cheesy slice on each. Very filling.

Avgolomeno Soup *For 4*

1 pint chicken stock	1 lemon
1 egg	

Heat the stock; beat up egg with the lemon. Pour a little of the hot stock into the egg–lemon mixture, and gradually add more; finally, tip this mixture back into the rest, but don't let it boil again. If you've got any cooked rice or vermicelli around, by all means add it – I never have.

For people out all day, the rule for having people to dinner is buy the first course, casserole the second have the last course cold and made the day before.

Jean Robertson

THE MAIN COURSE

or Only Poachers and Cookery Writers Need to Know How to Cook Rabbit.

Beef Casserole   *For 4–6*

1 lb braising steak
2 heaped tablespoons flour
2 teaspoons herbs – mixed, or marjoram, thyme or oregano
4 onions
2 tablespoons wine or old beer if possible
2 carrots
2 sticks celery
½ green pepper
2 oz mushrooms (optional)
2 tablespoons tomato paste
4 tomatoes (tinned or fresh)
1 crushed tooth garlic
1 teaspoon salt, pepper
2 tablespoons oil or dripping

Cut up the steak into bite-size pieces. Mix flour with herbs, salt and pepper and roll meat in it. Fry these in the fat till they change colour; take out of pan and fry onions, adding a bit more fat if necessary. Pour in wine and let it bubble. Then tip everything into a casserole, and cook at Reg. 2 (300F, 150C) for 3 hours. Check towards the end that there's enough salt.

As you might guess, you can change the vegetables around a bit – but don't end up back at school stew of carrot, turnip and swede.

Neptune Pie (fish pie fit for a king)   *For 4*

1 lb (or less) smoked haddock
3 medium onions
3 medium potatoes
3 tomatoes
1 teaspoon oregano or thyme or a mixture
2 oz flour
2 oz butter
½ pint milk
2 oz grated cheese
1 teaspoon salt
pepper

Chop onions, peel and dice potatoes; fry 10 minutes. Add tomatoes, herbs and seasoning, fry 5 more minutes. Meanwhile make sauce, melting butter, adding the flour, stirring in milk and finally the cheese. Pour onion mixture into shallow dish, break haddock into pieces and put here and there; pour sauce over and cook for 20 minutes at Reg. 5 (375F, 190C).

Corned Beef Hash   *For 4*

1 tin corned beef
4 onions
3 medium potatoes
1 tin tomatoes
1 teaspoon herbs
salt and pepper
1 crushed tooth garlic
dash of wine (optional)
oil for frying

Chop up onions and potatoes into dice. Fry these in 2 tablespoons of oil over medium flame until the potato is soft – about 10 minutes (you may need to add more oil). Now add the tomatoes and crush them up, add herbs, salt, pepper, garlic, and a dash of wine if you have it. Scrape the bottom of the pan as you go – there are nice crisp bits down there. Just 3 or 4 minutes before serving add a large tin of corned beef cut into chunks: it disintegrates if it goes in sooner.

Bistro Chicken Livers *For 2*

8 oz chicken livers
1 dessertspoon butter
1 dessertspoon oil
1 teaspoon mixed herbs or thyme
1 crushed tooth garlic

1 tablespoon brandy or whisky
5 oz single cream
1 teaspoon French mustard
salt, pepper

Pick over the chicken livers and remove any white or green bits. Melt butter and oil in a frying pan and cook the livers with the herbs and garlic for about 5 minutes – split one open to test, it should be *just* pink inside. Put them out of the pan on to a dish in a very low oven. Now put brandy in pan (it will hiss a bit); after a minute add the cream and mustard, salt, pepper; pour over the livers. Serve with rice or petits pois.

Pedro's Chicken *For 6*

6 chicken drumsticks
the same weight as the chicken of veal or pork fillet
1 onion
1 carrot

1 stick celery
2 teaspoons oregano or basil
olive oil for frying
salt, pepper
1 cup white wine

Fry chicken legs, and meat cut into smallish dice, until all has changed colour. Add finely-chopped vegetables, salt, pepper, herbs. Pour over a cupful of white wine and cook ¾–1 hour at Reg. 4 (350F, 180C) – it's done when you can easily spear the legs with a fork.

Bredin Bodge *For 6*
(or what happens when you cross moussaka with shepherd's pie)

1 lb mince
1 lb chopped onions
2 tins tomatoes
1 small tin tomato purée
salt and pepper
¼ lb grated cheese

1 oz butter
1 oz flour
1 pint milk
2 lbs potatoes peeled and sliced finely

Cook mince gently on low heat for 10 minutes; lift mince from pan and fry onions till soft – about 10 minutes. Add tomatoes, tomato purée, mince, salt, pepper; mix thoroughly. Make cheese sauce (see p. 15) melting the butter, stirring in flour, blending in milk; and then adding grated cheese.

Butter a big oven dish; put a layer of potatoes, a layer of meat mixture, a layer of potatoes and so on, finishing with potatoes. Pour over the cheese sauce. Cook at Reg. 4 (350F, 180C) for 1 hour, covered; then for another hour uncovered until potatoes are soft (test with fork).

Expatriate Goulash   *For 4*

2 big pork chops	1 tablespoon oil or dripping
2 tablespoons flour	½ tin tomatoes
2 teaspoons paprika	½ tin tomato purée
1 teaspoon mixed herbs	(2 tablespoons)
salt and pepper	1 cup water
3 onions	½ pot yoghurt
2 green peppers	

Cut the bone off those lovely pink chops, cut into chunks. Mix flour, paprika, herbs, salt and pepper. Roll meat in this. Fry onions and peppers in oil or (better) pork fat. Then fry the meat and add tomatoes, tomato purée and a cupful of water. Transfer all this to casserole (unless you were using a metal casserole anyway) and cook at Reg. 3 (325F, 160C) for 2 hours. Stir in yoghurt at last minute and serve with rice or packet potato dumplings.

In Hungary, goulash is actually a soup; but expatriate Hungarians are very adaptable.

Roast Chicken and All the Fixings

Sooner or later you're going to feel the urge to do this, if only to prove you can. The two things to remember are: (1) that you'll need at least a quarter of an hour *after* the chicken's done to fix the gravy etc. – it's safest not to tell them when dinner is to be; (2) because of the last-minute things, it's a great help to have some slow oven-cooked vegetable – see p. 44.

1 4-lb chicken	2 tablespoons dripping or
6 rashers bacon	butter
2 lbs potatoes	1 packet stuffing
1 packet Sainsbury's bread sauce	

Unfreeze the chicken thoroughly (overnight at least); light the oven to Reg. 6 (400F, 200C); put on a kettle for the stuffing, which has to sit for ¼ hour. Take the bag of innards out of the chicken, and put them with an onion and a carrot to boil for 20 minutes.

Stuff the stuffing in the chicken (it doesn't *matter* which end). Lay it in its tin with the rashers ranged across its bosom and the fat on top of that. Put it in the oven.

Peel 3 medium potatoes per person. When the fat round the chicken is melted (about ¼ hour) put them round the beast, spooning hot fat over them. Now go away and have a drink.

Get your vegetable in the oven, and spoon some fat over the bird – this should be done a couple of times while it's cooking.

Now grill sausages, if you want them, and more bacon, if you fancy it, and make the bread sauce. Check when the bird is ready, a 4-lb chicken takes about 1 hour 20 minutes. Shout for someone to set the table and start the final countdown.

10. Get bird on to carving dish, potatoes onto their dish, sausages, bacon, etc. round bird, all in the oven.
9. Turn oven down to Reg. 2 (300F, 150C), put in plates.
8. Shake up 2 tablespoons flour (preferably in flour-blender,

see page 31) with some of the stock you made by boiling the giblets.

7. Pour most of the fat out of roasting tin into a bowl, and place tin on medium high burner.

6. Pour in flour mixture and start stirring, adding more stock.

5. Keep stirring until all stock is added; if it still looks thicker than you'd like, go on adding water.

4. Add salt, pepper, and a spot of wine or old beer if you have it.

3. Find the carving knife.

2. Pour the gravy into a jug and put it in the oven.

1. Summon the family, get everything out of the oven and start carving.

When you can do this, you can do a **turkey** – it just cooks longer, and you shove sausage meat into its other end.

Cooking in foil means you don't have to spoon fat over – but put it *loosely* round the bird or it will just steam.

You can use a Roastabag if you loathe cleaning the roasting tin and the oven; but you can't do roast potatoes in its fat, and it's tricky getting the fat and juices out of the bag into a pan for the gravy.

Roasting Times

Meat	Degree of cooking	Time	Gas Reg.	F	C
Lamb	Well done	20 mins to the lb + 20 mins	6	400	200
	Beautifully pink	17 mins to the lb + 17 mins	6	400	200
Veal	Well done	20 mins to the lb + 20 mins	6	400	200
Pork	Well done (essential to kill all bacteria)	25 mins to the lb + 20 mins	6	400	200

Beef	Well done	20 mins to the lb + 20 mins	7	425	220
	Beautifully rare	15 mins to the lb + 15 mins	7	425	220
Chicken	Well done (very important – see instructions on p. 20)	20 mins to the lb	6	400	200

LEFTOVERS

Leftover Chicken Pie   *For 4*
(I only cook chicken so that I can make this with the leftovers)

1 packet frozen puff pastry
about 2 cups cooked chicken
2 onions
4 rashers bacon
1 crushed tooth garlic

6 mushrooms (optional)
1 tablespoon butter
2 tablespoons flour
¾ pint milk (or milk and water)

Start by taking out the frozen pastry – it'll take at least an hour to defrost. Chop up onions, bacon, garlic and mushrooms, if used, and fry gently for 15 minutes. While it's cooking, make a white sauce, melting the butter, adding the flour, gradually blending in the milk. Pour excess fat off onion mixture. Mix everything except pastry in a pie-dish; cover with the rolled-out pastry. Make a few slits in it, brush lightly with milk and bake it in Reg. 7 oven (425F, 220C) for 15 minutes.

Chicken Vol-au-Vent
If there's not enough chicken for a pie, make any scraps you have into a filling for vol-au-vent by making up the same mixture but without the bacon and onions. Use frozen vol-au-vent cases, or bought ones, or cut them out of rolled-out puff pastry.

Salad Soup
If you haven't eaten all the salad remains while you did the washing up, put them with a can of tomato juice in the blender. If makes a delicious cold soup.

Leftover Beef
Make corned beef hash recipe, p. 37, but add chopped-up beef at last minute instead of corned beef.

Leftover Casserole or Oeufs Bourguignonne (well, sort of)
Hard-boil (10 minutes) 2 eggs per person, heat remains of casserole and put eggs in, halved or whole.

Curry from Leftover Meat
Proceed as on p. 43 but put ½ teaspoon curry powder in when you add the tomatoes. More if you like your ears blasted off, but taste as you go.

Leftover Pork or Lamb Rissoles

For 4

2 cups diced cold meat with
  fat trimmed off
½ pint thick white sauce
  (1 tablespoon butter,
  2 flour)

nutmeg – salt – pepper
1 egg
packet breadcrumbs

Cut meat into small dice or mince it, season with salt and pepper. Make a thick white sauce by melting 1 tablespoon butter, mixing in the 2 tablespoons flour and gradually blending in ¼ pint milk, season with salt, pepper and nutmeg to taste. Combine the meat and the sauce, spread out on large plate until cold; it will stiffen into a rather nasty-looking congealed mass. Mould little sausage shapes or hamburger shapes; dip into beaten egg, then roll in breadcrumbs. Fry on a medium flame in cooking fat until brown on both sides.

Most **Leftover main dishes** can become little delicious first courses if you put them on small plates.

Leftover Fish

Flake it up with a fork, cook rice by Method 2 on p. 16, add 2 chopped-up hard-boiled eggs, a handful of raisins and 1 onion, raw, chopped very finely. Call it Kedgeree and hope for the best. If you happen to have a kipper about you, add that too.

Bacon Cakes

For 4

For the second half of a bacon joint, or any odd ends of bacon – good, bad or indifferent. Make up a packet of Sage and Onion Stuffing, following packet instructions. Put the bacon through the mincer; mix with stuffing; form into small flattish rissoles; dust with flour and fry in any old fat till golden brown – about 4 minutes a side.

Life is too short to stuff a mushroom.

Shirley Conran

What do you do if

your wife, who has been snuffling for days, develops a raging temperature and is whipped off to hospital, leaving you with three children to feed. Her parting words were 'there's the remains of the roast in the fridge'?

Involve the children: have the youngest set the table, send another down the road for a big tin of pea and ham soup and a packet cheesecake and have the third make up the cheesecake according to the directions on the packet.

Meanwhile you tackle 'that great hunk of sullen protein'. Cut off all the bits that look edible and chop them up fine. Put on a large pan to cook rice by Method 1 on p. 16 or, finding that you haven't got any, put 8 unpeeled potatoes in the water and boil for 20 minutes – they can jolly well peel their own. Now peel, chop and fry 3 onions in a couple of tablespoons of oil for 10 minutes over a medium flame, stirring them every now and then. Add 4 or 5 tomatoes, tinned or fresh; a tablespoon of tomato purée if you know where it is; any odd bits of vegetable that seem to be lurking in the fridge; ½ teaspoon of salt, several turns of the pepper mill and any herbs you can find. Finally add your meat – not sooner, or it will go tough.

Alternative Course (strongly recommended)
Put the children in the back of the car and drive round till you find a fish and chip shop.

A FEW FACTS ABOUT VEGETABLES

* Cats and dogs get along fine without eating any.
* The best way in the world to cook vegetables is the Chinese way, p. 60.
* There *are* healthful vitamins in potatoes.
* Most British vegetables are grown until they're too big and cooked until they're too soft.
* Petits pois in tins are delicious; petit pois frozen are a con – they are a dwarf variety and taste exactly the same as the bigger ones.
* The way to get skins off tomatoes is to pour boiling water over them for a minute or two; alternatively, hold them on a fork over a gas flame.
* The way to make sure you always have mushrooms is to dry them on paper on a plate on a radiator for a week, then put them in an air-tight jar – you only have to soak them for $\frac{1}{2}$ hour and they're ready for anything.
* Anything that grows under the ground – carrots, potatoes, celery, etc. can start in cold water and will take 15–20 minutes from the time the water boils.
* Anything that grows above should be dropped in boiling salted water and cooked for not more than 10 minutes.
(*Note*. The frozen packets cater to the national taste for sog – cut down the times they suggest.)
* Parsnips are not a food for human beings.

OVEN COOKED VEGETABLES

Cooking vegetables in the oven takes all the strain off the last 15 minutes before a meal and is usually delicious besides. **Baked potatoes** – huge brutes take 1 hour at Reg. 7 (425F, 220C) you can knock $\frac{1}{4}$ hour off this by putting them in the oven with a skewer through their centres. **Baked onions** should be peeled and rubbed in olive oil and salt; or put them with lump of butter in a parcel of foil. Take about the same time as potatoes. **Baked carrots** should be cut into strips about the size of half a pencil, part-boiled for 5 minutes and put in oven dish with 2 tablespoons water, dotted with 2 oz butter, sprinkled with a tablespoon sugar. Cook at Reg. 3 (325F, 160C) for an hour – or on the bottom shelf for longer while something else is cooking. Add salt and pepper *after* cooking. Even **frozen peas** are nicest if you put them, unfrozen, in a dish with a lump of butter, a sprig of mint, a teaspoonful of sugar and $\frac{1}{2}$ teaspoon salt on the lower shelf of an oven (where something else is cooking) for an hour.

Green Beans
Should be slender, and young, but shouldn't we all; in practice you are more likely to be stuck with big old runners. This is bad luck but do not despair. For each $\frac{1}{2}$ lb runner beans (or bobby beans) chop up 1 onion and fry it in a tablespoon of oil for 5 minutes. Then add the beans (you have peeled the strings from

44

down their sides) or your frozen packet; plus ½ tin (2 table-spoons) tomato purée and a large cup of water. If you have ore-gano or basil, add a teaspoon. Then let it stew for ½ hour at Reg. 4 (350F, 180C). (You can stew them slowly on the top of the stove too – same timings.)

Courgettes and Tomatoes
Allow 1 lb courgettes and ½ lb tomatoes for 6 people. Scrape the dark lines off the courgettes, slice off tops and tails and cut them into rounds. Fry them for 5 minutes in olive oil while you skin and roughly chop the tomatoes. Mix together with ½ teaspoon salt, pepper and a crushed tooth of garlic; cook at Reg. 4 (350F, 180C) for ¾ hour.

Red Cabbage
Allow ½ a small red cabbage for 6 people, plus 1 onion, 1 rasher of bacon if possible, 1 oz pork fat (or butter), 1 apple, ¼ teaspoon cinnamon, ¼ teaspoon cloves, 2 tablespoons vinegar. Chop up everything. Melt bacon and fat in heavy pot; fry onion for a couple of minutes, add everything else, transfer to oven and cook for 2 hours at Reg. 2 (300F, 150C). It can go on longer without risk.

Provençale Potatoes
Allowing 1 medium potato, 1 tomato and 1 onion per person, skin tomatoes (or open tin); chop up onions and fry for 10 minutes in oil. Add skinned tomatoes, crushed tooth of garlic, salt and papper. Peel and cut potatoes into thin slices. In a wide flattish dish put half the onion and tomato mixture, then the sliced potatoes, then the rest. Finish with half a dozen black olives if you have them – mainly for the look of the thing. Cook 1 hour at Reg. 6 (400F, 200C).

If you sprinkle 4 oz cheese over the top before cooking, this makes a supper dish on its own.

Ratatouille
2 onions	olive oil (essential)
1 aubergine or 3 courgettes	2 teeth of garlic, crushed
1 green pepper	1 teaspoon salt, pepper
3 tomatoes	2 teaspoons basil or oregano

In a big metal pot begin to fry the chopped onions as slowly as you can. After 10 minutes add the cut-up aubergines or cour-gettes; after another 5, the chopped peppers. Then the skinned tomatoes and everything else. Let it cook either in a low oven Reg. 2 (300F, 150C) or on top of the stove for at least an hour, preferably two. Heats up beautifully.

SALADS or 8 ways to avoid lettuce

I said long ago that my belief was that Persephone hadn't eaten anything in Hades when her mother arrived to fetch her home; 'Come back, dearest Persephone, and it will be forever summer!' said Ceres. 'So I have to wash lettuce all the year round?' said the suspicious girl. 'Pass me the pomegranates.' Lettuce is OK in a superb French dressing after a rather filling foreign meal, or in sandwiches; otherwise leave it to the rabbits.

Tomato Salad
Slice tomatoes, 1 per person; chop either 2 spring onions or a piece of regular onion very finely; pour over French dressing (p. 17) and add ½ teaspoon basil if possible. Can be made ahead.

Green Beans
Only super French beans (*not* ruddy runners) will do for this: boil 10 minutes; drain; put French dressing on while warm.

Bean Shoots
A bit boring on their own; splendid with a stick of celery chopped up with them, or an onion. Drop them into boiling water for about 2 minutes, drain, cover with dressing, and cool.

Waldorf Salad
1 cup diced apples (red skins look nicer)	1 cup chopped celery
	½ cup walnuts

Mix Hellmann's Mayonnaise with a tablespoon of plain yog-hurt, mix with juice of ½ lemon.

Cole Slaw
Bliss – but buy it.

Salade Niçoise
A meal in itself. Combine 2 tomatoes, half a dozen olives (black and/or green), ½ chopped-up green pepper, a small tin of tuna fish, ½ tin anchovies, 2 hard-boiled eggs, some broad or green beans (optional) and mix with 3 (or more) tablespoons of French dressing (p. 17). Main course for 2 or first course for 4.

Rice Salad
Cook a breakfastcupful of rice by Method 1 on page 16. Drain thoroughly. Now add: a slice of chopped ham, a finely-chopped onion, 4–6 green olives, 4–6 black olives, a dessertspoon of raisins or currants (optional), ½ chopped green (or red) pepper, 5–6 tablespoons of French dressing (p. 17).

This salad can be varied quite a bit; you can put in bits of celery or leftover meat or gherkins.

Red Bean Salad
Open a tin of red kidney beans, wash off the liquid in a strainer

under the tap; cut an onion into rings. Mix all this with 3 dessert-spoons French dressing, and avoid polite company.

PUDDINGS

You can go through life saying, 'I don't eat puddings' and making those who do feel like pigs – until you have to cook for someone else's children or, to be frank, men; who only pretend they have a soul above such things. Here are six which are dead easy.

Liz Ray's Apple Cream   *For 4*
1 lb cooking apples
1 oz (1 heaped
  tablespoonful) flour

4 oz (4 heaped tablespoons)
  sugar – preferably brown
1 5-oz pot single cream
1 teaspoon cinnamon

Peel the apples and cut them in chunks. Mix flour, sugar, cinnamon in a bowl; toss the apple chunks in this; put them in a flat dish and tip any remaining flour, etc. over them. Pour over the cream, cook at Reg. 5 (375F, 190C) for 35 minutes. Eat hot or cold.

Chocolate Mousse   *For 4*
4 eggs
1 large bar (200-g size) plain
  chocolate

1 orange
1 tablespoon rum (optional)

Separate yolks and whites of eggs. Grate and squeeze orange into saucepan; break up chocolate and melt all together over low flame. When melted, remove from flame and mix in yolks; add rum. Beat egg whites stiff and fold in gently. Chill. Without the rum it is less sticky, more suitable for children but not so delicious.

Boodle's Oodle Foodle   *For 4*
4 spongecakes (or leftover
  sponge)
6 oz double cream

2 oranges
1 lemon
1 tablespoon sugar

Beat the cream till it is only just beginning to be stiff. Add grated rinds and juice of oranges and lemon and the sugar. Mixture should be fairly liquid, but it depends on the fruit; if it's too thick, like porridge, add a little top of the milk. Arrange the spongecakes in a bowl and pour the fruity cream over them; leave to cool for 2 hours.

All millionaires love a baked apple.

Ronald Firbank

Summer Pudding (easy but takes 24 hours) *For 4*
1 lb blackcurrants or other
  soft fruit, bottled or frozen
bread

If you're using frozen or fresh currants, cook for 5 minutes with 2 tablespoons of sugar. Line a pudding basin with slices of crustless bread (*not* sliced blotting-paper); fill with currants, fit another piece of bread on the top; put a plate on it with a weight on top to force the juice into the bread; leave 24 hours. Even better using *Madeira cake* instead of bread.

Fruit Crumble

1 lb fruit – pears, apples,	8 digestive biscuits
even (I have to say)	3 oz butter
rhubarb	2 tablespoons sugar

Peel and cut up the fruit; if it's apple, add ½ teaspoon cinnamon and/or powdered cloves. Crush biscuits into crumbs and mix with melted butter. Put over fruit and cook for 35 minutes at Reg. 5 (375F, 190C). (If you're using eating apples, use only 1 tablespoon of sugar; you can stop as soon as they're soft when you prod with a fork.)

Apple Cornflake Bake *For 4*

2 lb eating apples	1 teaspoon cinnamon
2 large cups cornflakes	1 cup water
4 dessertspoons sugar	

Mix cornflakes, sugar and cinnamon together, peel and chop apples into chunks. Put alternate layers of apple and cornflakes, begin with apple, finish with flake, add water and cook at Reg. 5 (375F, 190C) for 30 minutes. Skip the sugar if you use Frosties. You can make a mountain of this in less time than it takes to write this out. (Good served with cream or ice-cream.)

Quick Puddings for Kids
If you're quite sure the grown-ups meant it when they refused pudding, go for these.

Ice Cream and Drizzle – The drizzle is chocolate sauce out of a tube, or a bar of chocolate melted – then it's hot as well, nice.

Blackbirds – Slices of bread fried for 5 minutes in butter over a medium heat, served with blackcurrant jam (and a spoonful of cream if you have it).

Brandy Snaps – Bought by the box, and filled with slightly whipped cream (or even Dream Topping).

Knickerbocker Glory – Ideal if you've a bit of leftover jelly and/or fruit. Compile a glassful per child of: jelly, ice cream, spoonful of jam, spoonful of fruit (or fruit salad), more jelly, more ice cream ...

And don't forget:
Marks and Spencer's Spotted Dick
Green's Packet Cheesecake
Bird's Angel Delight (butterscotch or peach flavours)
Jelly (for quick method, see p. 34)
Bought eclairs
Choc Ices
Fruit yoghurt
Banana mashed up with cream (or top of the milk).

Not Exactly a Pudding, But ...
* Petits Suisses served with black cherry jam.
* A fresh pineapple, cut carefully into rings (with or without kirsch).
* Peach salad – when peaches are cheap and/or bruised buy a bag of ripe ones, dip them in boiling water for a minute, peel and cut them up and add a little sugar, allowing one peach and a teaspoon of sugar per person.
* Kumquats in syrup – buy in a bottle from delicatessen.
* A plateful of Turkish delight and chocolates.
* Irish coffee – black, with sugar, cream and whisky.

What do you do if

you are told to prepare dinner for an overseas visitor, or someone else's new date, and it is Friday? Are they Catholic (in which case, no meat)? Are they Arabian (no pork, no booze)? Are they Jewish (no seafood, either, and watch the meat-and-milk)? No one, of course, thought fit to tell you – but it doesn't do to take chances.

Menu

Avocado Pear from Spain with French Dressing

Neptune Pie (see page 37)

Raspberry Mousse

Raspberry Mousse
Crush 1 lb raspberries; whip ½ pint cream. Crush 6 digestive biscuits, put on the bottom of a pudding dish, then the raspberries (plus sugar), then the cream; reserve a few raspberries for decorating. Of course they always may be diabetic, or the raspberry seeds may get stuck under their false teeth. But they can't have *everything*.

49

TEA

Afternoon tea as a meal fills me with gloom – it interrupts the afternoon, it's fattening and I'm not too struck on the actual liquid. But we can't get out of it all the time.

If you need to provide tea for children, don't panic – you don't need to bake – though the cake on p. 10 is dead easy if you've time. Buy a **cake** (my kids like Mr Kipling's Chocolate Fudge, Bird's Eye frozen sponge, Cherry Genoa or anybody's chocolate covered roll).

Lay out all the biscuits you can find on a big plate. Then organise something hot, which will make them feel they've had a great tea. For example:

Hot buttered toast – Put butter on as soon as toast is done.

Hot toasted tea cakes – Split and brown under grill.

Hot crumpets – Warm them (they don't actually need toasting), butter them and pile on top of each other.

Cinnamon toast – Mix $\frac{1}{2}$ teaspoon cinnamon with 2 dessertspoons sugar and 1 dessertspoon butter and spread on hot toast.

If you can manage to warm up some **small sausage rolls,** make **banana sandwiches** (mash up the banana, not just slice it) or cook some small **sausages on sticks,** they will love it (big sausages become little sausages if you carefully twist them in the middle). And don't forget **pain chocolat** – a little bridge roll with a couple of squares of chocolate in it.

If a thing's not worth doing at all, it's not worth doing well.
George Seddon

PICNICS

Picnics begin in the kitchen, more's the pity. But when you think of the best picnics you've ever had, the food was often not so difficult to make – just difficult to think of in the first place. Here are some suggestions taken from real, and excellent, outings.

Test Match Picnic
Each person was passed their share in a plastic bag so they didn't have to take their eyes off the game. In the bag:

Brown roll with butter and pâté in it

Small Marks and Spencer pork pie
A tomato

Later, slices of juicy fruit cake, cans of beer and apples were also handed along, and ingested, without anyone except me noticing any of it.

Scots River Picnic

Baps filled with scrambled egg and bacon (much better than hard-boiled)

Fried chicken drumsticks
Individual apple pies

French Beach Picnic

Corned beef hash kept warm
  in a vacuum jar
French bread and butter

Very ripe peaches
Sand

(The sand was unintentional; I put it in to remind you to take a plastic cloth.)

Local Horse Picnic

Quiche Lorraine (could have
  been bought)

Sticky apricots from a
  Health Food Shop eaten
  with cream cheese

This cheered a day in which host, hostess, their son and I think the son's horse all cowered with us in the back of a Mini. I need hardly say it rained throughout.

Cumberland Fell

Very classy picnics we have had in Cumberland; the lady who cooks them has wide horizons. She has given us:

Pieces of chicken cooked and
  wrapped individually in foil
Lamb Cutlets already cooked
  and seasoned well (she
  cuts off the fat)

Torpedo Sandwich – a long
  French loaf split down the
  middle with the inside
  taken out and replaced by:
  Ham – or Cheese – or
  Tomato – Mayonnaise-
  and-Lettuce. She says
  remember to bring a knife.

What not to have
Fish paste sandwiches
Dry bought sausage rolls
  (cold)
Very hard green apples
Tea put into Thermos with
  milk
Orange squash (warm)
Crisps

SANDWICHES

Sooner or later you will get stuck with sandwiches, because everyone likes eating them so – it's just making them that's a bore. Spread out all the slices edge to edge on a flat surface, and *get the butter soft* – it makes all the difference.

Fillings
Bacon (cooked), lettuce, tomato and mayonnaise
Cheese (Cheddar) and Branston pickle
Liver sausage and cucumber
Cottage cheese mixed with chopped spring onions
Smoked cod's roe and sliced cucumber
Cheese, apple and leek, first mixed in yoghurt
Corned beef and cole slaw
Tuna fish and mayonnaise and onion
Sardine and cream cheese in equal parts, mushed together.

SLIMMING IN THE KITCHEN

Look at any chef – let alone any chef's cat – and you'll see what the problem is: you cannot, as the Catholics say, avoid the occasion of the offence, and you have to taste things. How to avoid your waistline growing at the same pace as your confidence as a cook?

1. Have something around you *can* nibble safely – radishes, celery, raw cauliflower. It's the awful ease of biscuits that's the trouble.
2. Have the stodge part of the meal – the spuds, the rice – separate from the main protein part – meat and potatoes, not hash. Then *you* can have spinach instead.
3. Cut down the fat in cooking. *Slimming Magazine*, who toil night and day at this sort of thing, have a booklet that tells you how: for example, instead of frying onions for a spaghetti sauce and then adding the meat, you can brown the meat first in a non-stick pan and *then* add onions, pouring off excess fat at the end. Saves 400 calories a helping. Sit a joint on a rack for roasting (so it doesn't wallow in the fat), take the skin off a chicken (that's where its fat is). Make soup by putting vegetables and water in the blender and simmering the result. Shun mayonnaise and French dressing – mix yoghurt, salt, pepper and lemon juice instead. Crosse and Blackwell's Waistline helps, and so does Outline Low Fat Spread – for one thing it's so easy to say No to a second slice.
4. Cook when you're not hungry – in the morning, if possible; and only have one cooking session a day.
5. The best slimming aid is clingfilm, to cover the leftovers so that you can't nibble.

What do you do if

you realise that you have said 'Do bring the children' to two sets of people who are coming to Sunday lunch; not being a millionaire you have no desire to roast an ox, and can't quite remember how many children there are.

Menu

Spaghetti Bolognese (don't forget the Parmesan) as on p. 23.

Green Salad, with bits of cucumber and spring onion and perhaps watercress as well as lettuce.

Apple Cornflake Bake (p. 48) with Ice Cream.

Cheese

Lots of red wine and Coke

Alternative Solution

Keep the grown-ups in the living room while you hand round a tray of mezé (see p. 57). You have a casserole, say goulash, simmering in the oven. Meanwhile, let the children loose in the kitchen on a table set out with:

tomatoes, already sliced	slices of cheese
slices of ham	butter
hard-boiled eggs, already sliced	peanut butter
cucumber, already sliced	2 kinds of bread
bottled mayonnaise	Branston pickle

and let them compile their own sandwiches *without adult supervision*. Probably it's this last which makes this such a popular option.

When they've finished, you sweep the mess aside and give the grown-ups their casserole, finishing with fruit and cheese.

PART SIX

Branching out

A SUMMER MEAL FOR FOUR

Cold Mint Soup

Anchovy Veal with Ratatouille

Strawberries and Cream

Cold Mint Soup
Several hours ahead, peel half a cucumber and chop it into matchstick-sized pieces. Mix 2 pots plain yoghurt with ½ pot single cream and a crushed clove of garlic (important) plus about a tablespoon of finely-chopped fresh mint. Add the cucumber, and if you can manage it 4 oz shrimps. Put in a cool place, and sprinkle a little more mint at the last minute.

Anchovy Veal
First mash ½ tin anchovies with 1 oz (1 dessertspoon) butter. Cut crusts off 4 slices of bread and fry them till golden brown in a mix of oil and butter. Spread the anchovy butter over them and put in a low (Reg. 1, 275F, 140C) oven on a flat dish. (The ratatouille – made beforehand as on p. 45 – is already keeping warm there.)

Now take 4 small veal escalopes (or pieces of flash-fry veal), hit them hard with a meat tenderiser or the heel of a bottle; fry 2 minutes each side over medium heat in oil and butter (they're done when a fork goes easily in). Put them on the fried bread. Pour a glassful of white wine into the pan, add another lump of butter and pour that over the lot. It's delicious.

AN AMERICAN BRUNCH

Forget your tirade about the decline of the English language and arrange to eat this excellent transatlantic spread. None of the brunch things is difficult. I'm supposing you have about 8 people for a summer Sunday (so it may well rain). Set out all the breakfasty crockery on a table for people to help themselves – silver candlesticks would look idiotic.

You should aim to offer:

One fruit dish – say dried apricots soaked overnight and boiled for 20 minutes with fresh apples and pears.

One main dish – sausages and scrambled eggs, and corn fritters (p. 25); or corned beef hash (p. 37); or bacon cakes and beans (p. 42).

Hot rolls, or hot crumpets or hot muffins.
An exotic marmalade and/or jam – ginger marmalade, blueberry jam, or honey.
Coffee.

I was so darned sorry for poor old Corky, I didn't have the heart to touch my breakfast. I told Jeeves to drink it himself.

P. G. Wodehouse

Some sort of alcohol that passes for juice so you can start well before the sun is over the yard-arm – try Bucks Fizz which is 2 parts champagne (i.e. Veuve de Vernay or other supermarket fizz) to 1 orange juice; Bloody Mary (3 parts tomato juice to 1 vodka, plus a dash of Worcester sauce and a slice of lemon) or Gin and Grapefruit – gin, juice and soda water in whatever proportions you think prudent – I drink it 1 to 1 to 1.

What do you have when

the woman who always waves her hips at your husband comes to dinner?

Harengs Marinée made by de-skinning uncooked kippers, cutting them into little strips and marinating them in French dressing with rings of raw onion and a bay leaf for 24 hours. Undeniably delicious, but ...

Pedro's Chicken (p. 38) with **Tomato Courgettes** (as on p. 44 but with a double load of garlic).

A fresh orange salad – oranges skinned and sliced, with sugar; with any luck she'll get bits of pith between her teeth.

It'll take a hell of a lot of Arpège to drown that lot. And if you put the chicken dish in the oven as the bell rings, there'll be no need at all to leave the sitting room for prolonged periods – or even a couple of minutes.

A SPANISH DINNER FOR SIX

Gazpacho

Paella

Ripe Peaches

Gazpacho

2 tins tomatoes
½ onion
½ (or less) pimento
3 tablespoons olive oil
1 tablespoon vinegar
1 tooth garlic
¼ teaspoon salt
pepper

For serving
6 black olives
2 hard-boiled eggs
¼ cucumber or more
green pimento
2 slices of bread for croûtons

Put all the first set of ingredients through the blender and put it in the fridge (or a black cellar) to cool. Then you prepare the croûtons as on p. 35, chop up the eggs, cucumber, etc. which you hand round separately in little dishes at table. If you haven't a blender, you can of course chop everything madly, which is more authentic but takes longer.

Paella

½ lb peas
½ lb French beans
2 green peppers
2 tablespoons oil
¼ lb cooked chicken
¼ lb pork fillet or ham or bacon
2 scallops or ¼ lb shrimps
1 onion, chopped
2 cloves garlic, chopped
2 tomatoes, peeled and quartered

½ lb rice
bouquet garni
1 teaspoon turmeric to colour
2 pints stock
¼ lb scampi or prawns
6 smoked mussels
cayenne pepper
salt and pepper

This is best made in a deep pan which can be used for frying and also go in the oven. Failing this, the ingredients can be transferred from a frying pan to a casserole.

Fry the peas and beans and the chopped peppers; keep them hot. Melt the oil, brown the diced chicken and pork/ham/bacon in it. Add the sliced scallops or shrimps, the onions and the garlic. Fry until the onions are golden, add the tomatoes, the rice, the bouquet garni, the turmeric and the stock. Simmer for 10 minutes.

Arrange the scampi/prawns and the mussels on top. Cook in a hot oven Reg. 7 (425F, 220C) for 10 minutes. Add the peppers, peas and beans and serve directly from the cooking pot.

A GREEK LUNCH FOR SIX

Mezé

Papoutsakia

Tomato Salad

Greeks like to go on drinking, so they are good at nibbles – mezé is the word. Hand it round instead of a first course. Include some or all of these:

Black olives; slices of salami; quarters of tomatoes; quarters of hard-boiled egg; pieces of cheese (the tougher, older and whiter the more authentic, but don't bother about *that*); shrimps; vine leaves stuffed with rice (comes in a tin).

If you want to start right in, serve bought taramasalata with that flat Greek bread called pita which, thanks to the troubles in Cyprus, you can now buy in most towns.

Papoutsakia

Scrape the ridges off 2 lbs of courgettes and slice off tops and tails. Drop them in boiling water for 10 minutes. Meanwhile fry 2 medium onions (chopped) and ½ lb mince; when the mince has changed colour add a dessertspoon of tomato paste, salt, pepper and a teaspoonful of oregano (or basil). Slice the courgettes lengthways, lay them on a flat dish and pile the mince on top.

Now make a cheesy sauce by melting 2 oz of butter, blending in 2 oz of flour and 1 pint milk; stir in 2 heaped tablespoons of grated cheese and half a teaspoonful of salt. Pour this all over everything else, and bake it at Reg. 4 (350F, 180C) for 15 minutes.

If your guests, fortified by their mezé, won't come to table at the end of the quarter of an hour, just turn the oven right down until they're ready – it won't spoil.

Serve the tomato salad either with or after this, and some fresh fruit – Greeks aren't good on puddings anyway.

What do you do if

a Special Friend is coming for dinner? You don't want to look as if you've *tried* – but of course it must be delicious; and not too heavy, if you hope for a session on the sofa later. The one thing not to do is to give him the sort of meal he might get at a business lunch.

Hell's Angels

Ham and Chicory Gratin

Cold Green Beans in French Dressing

Peaches in White Wine

Hell's Angels are tinned smoked mussels or oysters with half a rasher of streaky bacon wrapped round each, grilled on a skewer 5 minutes each side, allowing 6 to each skewer.

Ham and Chicory Gratin. Wrap heads of chicory in slices of ham and cover with a cheese sauce made by melting 2 oz butter, adding 2 oz flour, blending ¾ pint milk, plus a spoonful of white wine, salt and pepper; cook at Reg. 4 (350F, 180C) in a flat dish for 20 minutes or until chicory is soft. It can safely sit at the bottom of the oven keeping warm.

Skin **peaches** as for tomatoes (p. 43), cut into slices and put into 2 wine glasses with a little of the white wine you are serving with the dinner poured over them.

What not to give him

Elaborate hors d'oeuvre

A big steak, overdone and tough

Fried potatoes, whose smell lingers in your hair

A lovingly prepared gateau weighing 4 tons

A CHINESE DINNER FOR FOUR

Peking Hot-Sour Soup
Beef and Bean Sprouts
Chop Suey
Soy Rice

Most Chinese cooking is done very quickly and served immediately. So you have an obvious problem for the cook who is
also proposing to eat the stuff. The solution is to balance your
menu so that you don't have too much to do at the last minute.
You might do a cold first course of Chinese meats and pickles,
if you can get them, but in this one you can make the soup early
in the day and just heat it up at the end. Rice keeps hot for a
long time, and in a slightly warm oven will manage for half an
hour without drying. Hotplates down the centre of the table
could keep the other dishes alive. But the vital thing is that,
before you go into the last 10 minutes of cooking, you have the
ingredients properly chopped, measured, blended and whatnot
so that you just reach for a cup or bowl and heave it into the
pan.

The only exotic ingredients needed are soy sauce and bean
sprouts – preferably fresh, but if tinned, soak them in cold water
for half an hour before cooking.

Peking Hot-Sour Soup

2 pints weak chicken stock:
   made from cubes will do
2 sliced mushrooms
1 tablespoon vinegar
1 dessertspoon soy sauce

salt and pepper
1 egg, beaten
(a few scraps of cooked
   chicken or ham if you
   have them)

Simmer the mushrooms in the stock for 2 minutes. Add everything else except the egg and simmer another 2 minutes. You
can then let it cool and work on other dishes. At the last moment
before serving, bring to the boil and pour the beaten egg in over
the back of a spoon; this should produce an instant covering
of tiny shreds of egg, which adds more to the texture than to
the taste.

Beef and Bean Shoots

1 lb braising or chuck steak
¾ lb bean shoots, or 1 largish
   tin (the quantity isn't vital)
2 tablespoons sherry
1 tablespoon soy sauce
½ tablespoon sugar
1 dessertspoon cornflour
   (mixed with a little water)

salt
1 egg white
2 tablespoons oil
the fine-grated rind of a
   largish orange (this is
   vital)

Freeze the beef. When it is almost frozen or just getting unfrozen,
it is far easier to slice small. Cut it into thin slices downwards,
then cut these into 'matchsticks' lengthways. You should end up
with it cut slightly thinner than a pencil and about half as long.

Mix all the other ingredients except the orange peel, then marinade the beef in them for a few hours (the cheaper the beef, the longer the marinade) stirring occasionally.

When ready to cook, drain off most of the marinade and keep.

Put a little oil in a hot frying pan and 'stir-fry' the bean shoots for 2 minutes. This simply means stirring them around over a fairly high heat. Take the bean shoots from the pan. Add a little more oil if it seems needed, and stir-fry the beef and the grated orange peel until the beef has turned colour. Throw in the bean shoots and the rest of the marinade and cook for another 2 minutes, or less.

Chop Suey

Supposedly invented by Chinese cooks on the American railroad construction teams, this is nevertheless a good vegetable dish.

¼ lb white or Chinese cabbage, chopped into something like 1-inch squares salt	1 dessertspoon soy sauce a couple of tablespoons of stock or just water (you could pirate some of the soup for this)

After that, choose two or three of the following:

a grated carrot spring onions, chopped, using most of the green stalk as well an ordinary onion, chopped coarsely a stick of celery, chopped into half-inch slices	a couple of mushrooms, sliced a few bean shoots (if you have any left over from the beef dish)

Stir-fry the solider vegetables – onions, celery, carrot – for about 5 minutes in a little oil. Then put in the softer ones – bean sprouts, mushrooms, spring onions – for another 2 minutes, then add stock, soy, a sprinkle of salt and simmer for another few minutes. The key is to get the cabbage and onion looking translucent but still crisp to the taste. You won't go wrong by under-cooking.

Soy Rice

Do a cupful of rice by Method 2 (p. 16) and then, when it is cooked, stir in a tablespoon of chopped spring onions and a tablespoon of soy sauce.

The rice will keep warm in its cooking pot for at least a quarter of an hour while you get on with the last-minute things.

A SCOTTISH HIGH TEA
(just about no cooking)

Smoked mackerel
Oatcakes
White bread
Ginger cake
Raspberry jam
Strong tea

None of this needs cooking except the mackerel, which should be warmed up for 5 minutes in a low oven, Reg. 2 (300F, 150C). The best tea I've ever eaten consisted of all this, eaten in any old order, plus whisky, on the boat on which we'd just caught and smoked the mackerel. You could add shortcake if you're feeling affluent.

What do you do if

you are kicking around in the flat having just shampooed your hair when your flatmate rings to say she is bringing home not one but two delightful young men, how about some supper?

Get your rollers out for heaven's sake.

Clear up the flat a bit.

Check that there is *something* to drink, if it's only ginger wine.

Put on something you look good in, and then see what there is in the store cupboard. Don't aim to make more than *one dish* even if (amazingly) there seem to be several things: you won't have time.

Switch off the brighter lights and try not to look desperate as they come through the door.

If you know you've always got enough of it, you've just run out of it.

Gavin Lyall

INDEX

SOME LIKE IT . . . .

DE-FREEZING TIMES

Joints, packets of mince etc.	Overnight
Chicken	Overnight, without its paper. Check it's completely defrozen and run hot water into its innards if not – incompletely thawed chicken is dangerous.
Paté, Fish paté etc	1-2 hours
Bread	15 mins in a hot oven 2 hours otherwise

A slice of bread de-freezes in 10 minutes, and can be put into a toaster straight from frozen

Fruit	About 2 hours ; break it up as soon as it begins to be crunchy
Casseroles	Ideally, overnight. But you can run the container under the hot tap to get out the casserole, and start it off in the oven; it's better thawed slowly, but this way you can get it ready to eat in two hours.
Frozen Pastry	At least one hour